Trace over the lines to help the tractors reach the bales of hay.

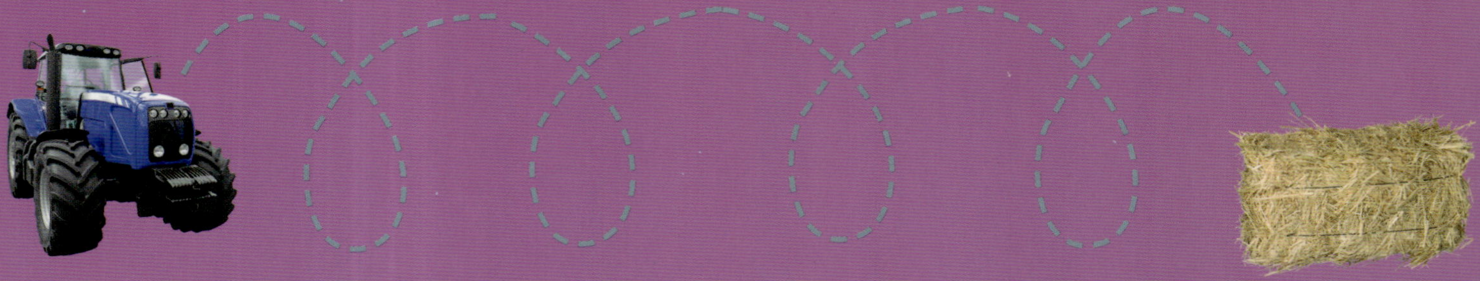

Trace over the missing letters to complete the words.

Digger Digger

Puff puff!

Trace the line around the digger.

Trace over the missing letters to complete the words.

Digger Digger

Well done!

Ff Ff   Gg Gg

Trace over the lines to draw the fence.

Trace over the missing letters to complete the words.

Digger Digger

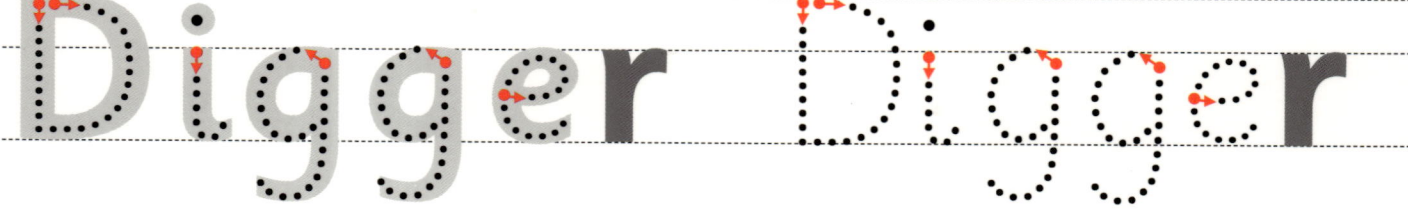

Chug chug!

Hh Hh   Ii Ii

Find the three differences between the two pictures and circle them.

Well done!

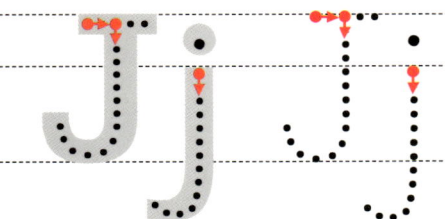 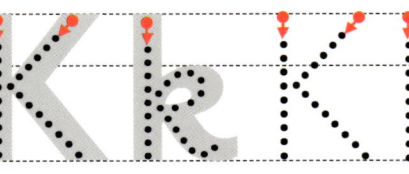

Help the tractor find its way to the barn.

Draw lines to match up the diggers to their buckets.

Pp Pp   Qq Qq

Trace the lines to finish off the digger.

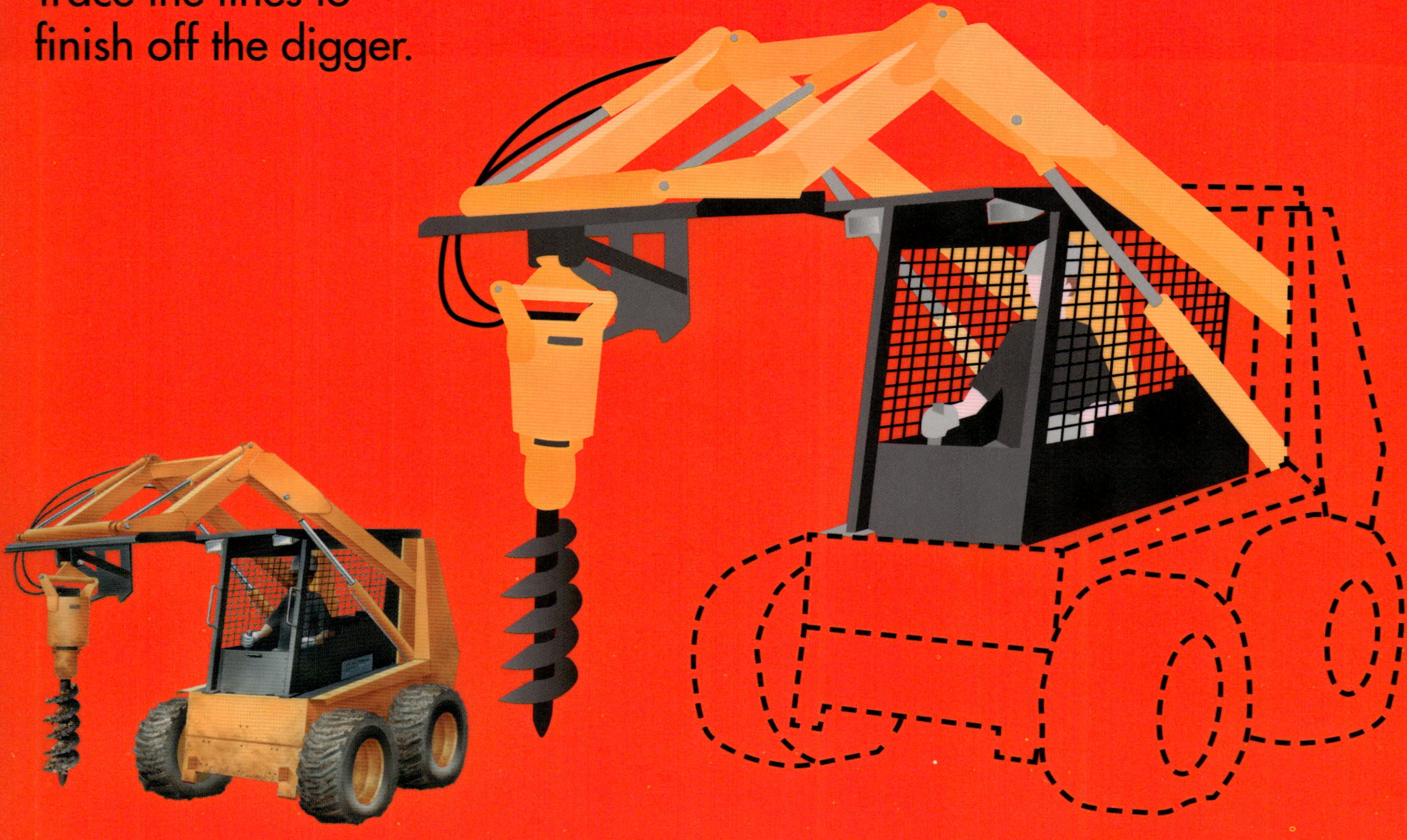

Trace over the missing letters to complete the words.

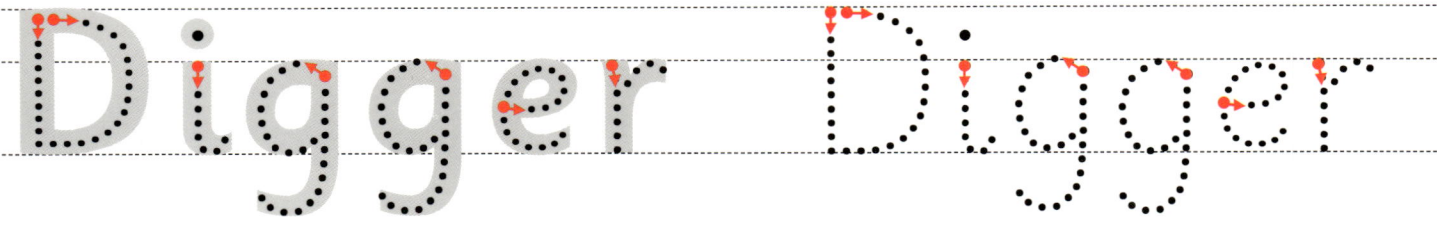

Well done!

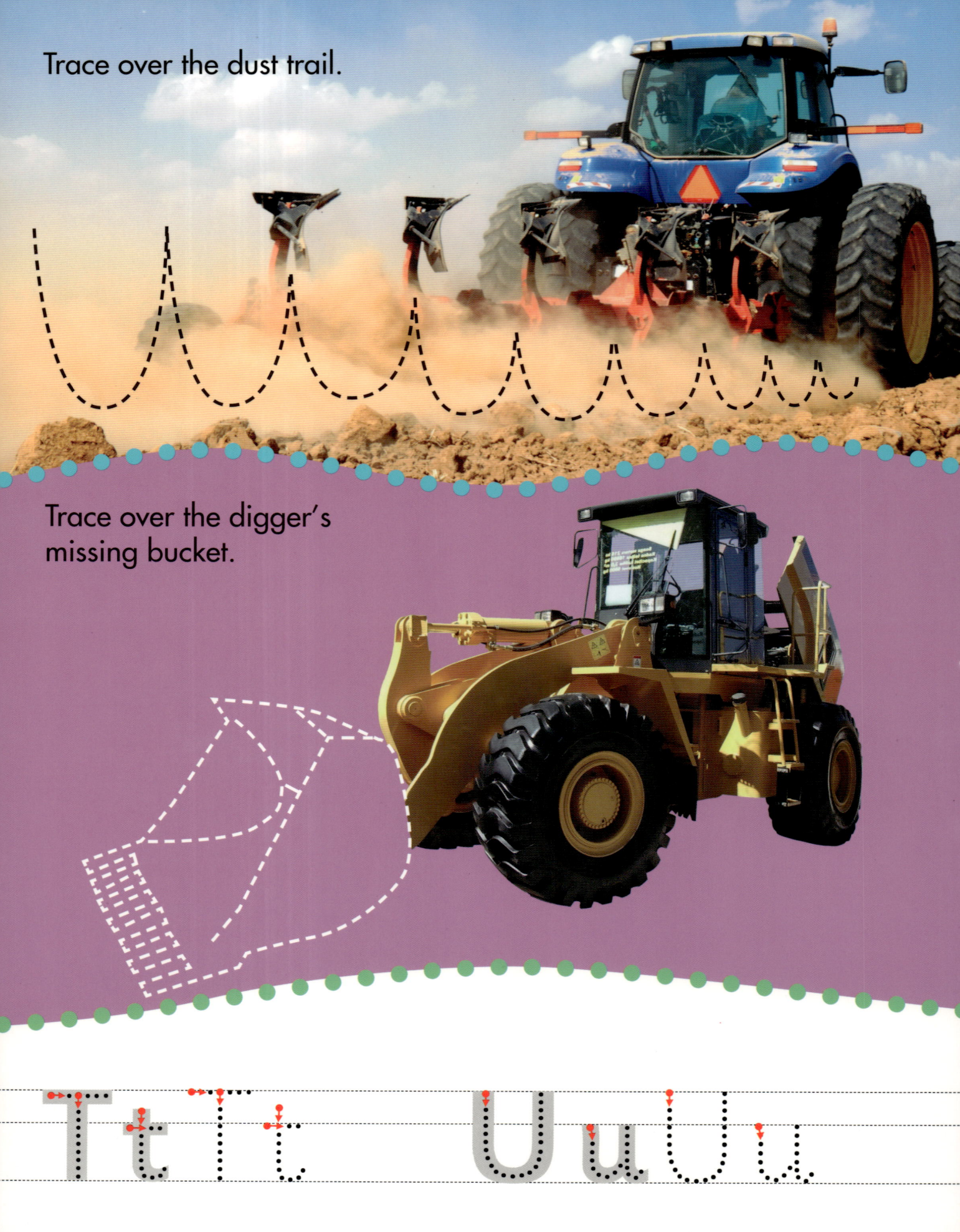